Same ported hand-stripes. ancies. orings. n will

$1.30

medi-ations rsians, res and wines, shades. Don't of the ...38c.

w Pull rench in 50 checks. d dark band e ends, ned or i. The icatest. dozen nted or

...75c.

Fine and s, 100

..65c.

arfs.

2.

Pure House ny new ding at ations. dens, gures. signs. rming styles. ᴋ or mber pure

No. 21575 Children's Fancy Parasols. Made in new and beautiful patterns; light colors, like pink, blue, etc. Size, 10 inch..$0.17
Size, 12 inch..............22
Size, 14 inch.............33
No. 21576 This is an exceptionally nice Misses' Sateen Parasol; 14 inch., plain solid colors, with ruffle, fancy stained and polished handles; colors, pink, cardinal, white, or blue.
We offer this at an exceptionally low price, and guarantee it to give perfect satisfaction.
Our special price $0.48

Misses' Fancy Foulard Pattern Paarasol.

No.21577 Large choice assortment of handsome patterns; floral and dresden designs, etc., new and beautiful colorings. Nicely made and finely finished throughout; natural wood handles. Our special prices,
1¼ inch.............$0.50
16 inch.................76

THIS IS A VERY HANDSOME

16 IN. MISSES'

FANCY FOULARD... PATTERN PARASOL.

No. 21578 with a beautiful star ruffle of satin, corresponding in color to that of the parasol. Handsome shades of light blue and pink. Newest fancy patterns; natural wood han-dles; nicely made and finished.
Our special price...................87c

THIS IS AN

EXCEPTIONALLY FINE....

MISSES' PURE ...SILK...

PARASOL.

No. 21579 Has deep flounce and puff. Extra fine quality natural wood sticks. Size 14 inch. Made in plain colors only; pink, blue and cardinal. Extra made and nicely finished. Guaranteed to please the most sceptical.
Our Special Price...................$1.10

IF THE COST OF THE BOY'S CLOTHING

See our special half-dozen offer. It will pay you to lay in a supply for yourself and friends.
No. 2224. Men's Fine Fancy Silk Teck Scarfs. The kind that you usu-ally pay 35c, 45c, and 50c for. Our price is a revelation. We buy di-rect, thousands of dozens at a time, around. These scarfs are made fr imported fancy silks. We have th stripes, dots, neat figures, and in medium and dark combination co black or white. All nicely made Surprising values, every one of the price, each...........19c; Six for....

Silk Folding or String T

Fancy Figured Silk String T
No. 2225. Medium width, assorted, dark or medium colors, nicely made and finely finished folded string ties.
Per dozen.... 2.50 Price, each.. $0.23

Black Silk Folded Ties.

Known as string ties, made of pure gros grain silks, extraordinary values in each number; this is a tie that can be worn on all occasions, and especially suitable for elderly gentlemen.
No. 2226. ⅝ inch wide...14c each...6 for $0.80
No. 2227. ¾ " " ...18c each..6 for 1.00
No. 2228. ⅞ " " ...22c each..6 for 1.25
No. 2229. 1 " " ...27c each..6 for 1.55
No. 2230. 1½ " " ...30c each..6 for 1.75

Hot Weather Neckwear
An untied man i. ever an untidy man. No chance for untidiness here. Ours is a tide of low prices and should be taken at the flood.

Gentlemen's Silk Bow Ties.
For turn-down Collar.

No. 2232. Fancy Silk Bow Ties for 6 cents, with shield for turn-down collar. Any of this lot of ties would cost you a quarter in any retail store. There is nothing old or off-color; everyone is as hand-some as can be; all full size, pretty fancy colors; made of remnants of silks. We have con-tracted to take all the largest manufacturer of neck ties in New York will have for the entire season. They are made from remnants left from high grade ties, and are a bargain.
Each....................6c
¼ doz., assorted........30c

No. 2246. Black Silk Bows, with shield and elastic loop for turn-down collar,
Each......10c; ½ dozen, for.....50c
No. 2250. Men's Fine Black Satin Bows, with shield and elastic loop, for turn-down collars. Extrafine se-lected stock. Price, each........10c;
6 for 50c

Black Band Bows.
For Standing Collar.
No. 2251. Black Bow. Pop-ular wedding tie, fine grade satin and silk. Each.... .. 15c
Half doz.....................80c
No. 2252. Same as above, only pure white. Each. ..15c

No. 2251.

Half doz........80c.
No. 2254. Sena-tor Band Bow. Extra quality silk or satin, lat-est shape, with patent band clasp at back so it can be worn with standing collar. Plain black only.
Each... ....15c Half dozen......80c

White China Silk Band Bows.
No. 2255. Men's Extra Fine Pure White China Silk Band Bows for standing colars.— The daintiest

satin ribbon, satin ribbon.
Each.........

LADIES' MOURNING BONNET.

No. 23479 We show in this illustration a very handsome Bonnet and Mourning Veil. It is made exactly like the cut, of extra quality material. We of-fer it as an especial bargain and its actual value is at least 50 per cent. above our prices if bought in retail stores.
Our special price........$2.98

NOTE.—When ordering trimmed hats kindly tion color that is wanted.

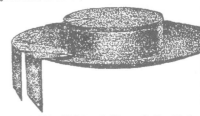

Untrimmed Hats.

Our Line of Untrimmed Hats was never complete at the beginning of a season than now. We have everything that is new and st and the prices are lower than ever. It is well member that many a dollar can be saved by b your hats of Sears, Roebuck & Co.

No. 23481 Children's Straw Sailor Hats, r around band and ribbon streamers in the Colors, navy, brown, cardinal and black. Th is usually sold by retail merchants at from 30c.
Our special price, each.................

No. 23483 Charlotte, a new straw shape lik but made of a rough straw; this hat will be very ionable this spring. Colors, black, white and Each................

No. 23484 Ladies' Black or White "Le

Manners and Customs

LIFE IN AMERICA 100 YEARS AGO

Manners and Customs

Jim Barmeier

Chelsea House Publishers
New York   Philadelphia

CHELSEA HOUSE PUBLISHERS
Editorial Director: Richard Rennert
Executive Managing Editor: Karyn Gullen Browne
Copy Chief: Robin James
Picture Editor: Adrian G. Allen
Creative Director: Robert Mitchell
Art Director: Joan Ferrigno
Production Manager: Sallye Scott

LIFE IN AMERICA 100 YEARS AGO
Senior Editor: Jake Goldberg

Staff for **MANNERS AND CUSTOMS**
Editorial Assistant: Erin McKenna
Senior Designer: Basia Niemczyc
Picture Researcher: Sandy Jones
Cover Illustrator: Steve Cieslawski

First Printing

1 3 5 7 9 8 6 4 2

Library of Congress Cataloging-in-Publication Data

Barmeier, Jim.
    Manners and Customs / Jim Barmeier.
    p. cm.—(Life in America 100 years ago)
    Includes bibliographical references and index.
    Summary: Discusses life in the United States around the turn of the twentieth century
    in such areas as work and leisure, clothing and fashion, and courtship and marriage.
    ISBN 0-7910-2844-5
    1.United States—Social life and customs—1865–1918—Juvenile literature.
[1. United States—Social life and customs—1865–1918.] I. Title. II. Series.
E168.B25 1996   95-24735
391'.00973'09034—dc20   CIP

                                                                                 AC

CONTENTS

LIFE IN AMERICA 100 YEARS AGO

Frontier Life

Health and Medicine

Industry

Law and Order

Manners and Customs

Sports and Recreation

Transportation

Urban Life

Manners and Customs

Work and Leisure

AS AMERICA ENTERED ITS SECOND CENTURY AS A NATION, the work style of its populace was undergoing an enormous transformation. The agricultural roots that had nurtured the country in its first hundred years were withering. In their place were the smokestacks and factories of industry. Life on the family-owned farm, long the backbone of the economy, was changing as rural people came to depend on the goods and services of a rapidly expanding industrial and commercial base. As the population grew, more from immigration than births, demand for goods and services grew and many small businesses were evolving into big companies, complete with assembly lines, managers and foremen, time cards, and new theories about worker productivity and efficiency. By the start of the 20th century, more than two-thirds of the country's nonfarm work force were employed in large factories. Whole towns and cities evolved around single industries such as steel and textiles.

The Fourth of July celebration in Madison Square, New York City. 1876 With the Civil War over, the country experiencing rapid industrialization, and millions of new citizens coming in from Europe and elsewhere, people had a sense that the nation was undergoing a vast transformation.

The biggest changes came in work habits. The factories required that people adapt their work rhythms to those of the new machines, which ran continuously at an even pace. Workers unused to a factory lifestyle found themselves in a world that was more mechanized, impersonal, and disciplined. A worker no longer had the luxury of smoking or singing on the job, of planning his own breaks, or of varying the type of work he was engaged in to eliminate boredom. Now the worker had to conform to the rules and the culture of the factory, where time was measured in dollars of output. Industry was moving rapidly toward regular, standardized mass production.

Industrial work lacked variety. Each day's work schedule consisted of a series of repetitive tasks that had to be finished as quickly as possible. Time clocks appeared in factories to regulate promptness. This created a sharper distinction between work and leisure time. The slower, more casual work style of the early craftsman gave way to the frantic rush to increase output, and people began to take more seriously their time away from the office or assembly line. More people than ever before were able to enjoy a variety of activities. The habit of taking a vacation, a privilege once reserved for the wealthy, began to spread to the middle class. Resorts appeared in Atlantic City and in Florida. During the last decades of the 19th century, physical fitness became a craze. Exercise classes were introduced into schools. John Harvey Kellogg and C. W. Post began the breakfast-food industry. Roller-skating and bicycling became popular. Professional sports events made their appearance, as did the soda fountain, the amusement park, the vaudeville house, and the country fair.

The work world became a power struggle between workers and employers. Workers did not want to lose their individuality or their

11

identity. Employers wanted to control time and productivity. The late-19th-century worker struggled to protect and promote himself in the face of a changing industrial America. Labor Day became a national holiday in 1894, celebrating the contributions of the American worker through parades and pageants. Protests and boycotts were made to improve factory conditions or to raise wages. The most dramatic means of protest was the strike, a direct response to employer authority. As an index of the tension between labor and management at the time, over 7 million workers were involved in approximately 37,000 strikes in the last quarter of the 19th century.

Going hand in hand with the expansion of industry in the late 19th century was the evolution of the modern office. Small businesses were turning into big, national corporations, and bureaucracies were needed to manage them. The first skyscrapers sprang up in urban centers in the 1880s to house the central home offices of major corporations and to provide prestigious locations for big business.

Several features highlight the birth of the office bureaucracy. The first was the shift in gender composition of the office staff. Before the 1870s, most offices were small and administered by men. Office work was held in high esteem and the male "clerks" were paid respectable wages. By the end of the century, however, the makeup and status of office jobs had changed. Office workers were now considered part of the clerical staff, more than a third of which was composed of women. Often, female graduates of high school—itself a new innovation—had taken commercial courses or had attended one of the budding business schools. These women turned to office work because few other opportunities, except nursing and teaching, were available. Women office workers made a third more than their counterparts in teaching and more than twice as much as women

From the 1830s onward, workers agitated for shorter working hours, and by the 1860s the eight-hour workday had been recognized by law. Although millions of Americans still worked six-day weeks, the limitation of hours gave citizens more leisure time to pursue personal interests.

working in mills. The chance for advancement was small, however, because pay and promotion scales still favored men. A woman—usually white, native born, young, and single—might become a department head or supervisor, but never anything higher.

The second innovation in offices was the introduction of new technology and business practices. The typewriter made its appearance in the 1870s. Black and sturdy in design, it was promoted by manufacturers as ideal for women because of their "nimble fingers." This sort of stereotyping led to the employment of growing numbers of women in typist positions well into this century. Complementing the typewriter was the new flattop office desk, as well as standardized desk arrangement and identical worker equipment. The dictaphone was also devised in 1885.

Modern work could be monotonous and degrading, but with machine power the brute strength of male workers became less important, and millions of women entered the work force.

With the growth of bureaucracies in American business came the need for a new class of managers. The new industrial managers were educated and innovative. Management procedures became systematic, or scientific, following the new field of social engineering. This new business philosophy promoted time savings, centralized planning, constant supervision, and wages based on company conformity. In both the factory and the office, workers were made to feel like the machines they were operating—each movement controlled, each detailed operation under review.

The final major difference between the work world of the pre-1870s and the following 30 years was the introduction of women into the work force. In the mechanized factory, women frequently were hired more often than men because they were thought to be both responsible and trouble-free. Twenty percent of the mill workers in 1900 were women. The number of female domestic workers declined from half the total female work force in 1870 to only one-sixth by the early 1900s. Government employment also opened up for women. Almost a third of all federal clerks in 1900 were women.

The world of leisure activity was also experiencing a real transformation. Americans were beginning to realize that they did not have to spend their entire lives working, and they started to have fun with new forms of recreation. Whole businesses were created to cater to leisure activities. Engineering innovations brought the country the bicycle and the amusement park.

Men and women of all economic classes participated in this revolution in leisure activities. The traditional notion of how to use one's spare time—principally for self-improvement, in the best tradition of the work ethic—was being challenged. Certainly, free time should be used to expand the mind and improve the body, but it could also be simply pleasurable.

The majority of Americans could not afford to spend much time away from work, so recreation was limited to evenings or weekends. Organized events predominated. For the family, there were church socials, picnics, lawn games, parlor gatherings, club activities, and holiday outings. Lawn tennis and croquet could be played outside, while the parlor organ and piano provided indoor music socials in the evenings. Young girls had their needlecrafts. Young boys enjoyed the stories of Tom Swift and The Hardy Boys. Anxious to find common interests, many Americans joined clubs and associations, often known by some odd names such as the Independent Order of Gophers or the United Order of Druids. By the turn of the century, almost half of the male population belonged to these new clans or lodges.

Vacations were being redefined. Middle-class Americans expected to be given a paid vacation, although blue-collar workers were not quite so lucky. Summer breaks were common for the middle-class worker. When they did take a break, professionals generally went to Europe on transatlantic crossings, indulged themselves at health spas, visited Victorian resorts, or spent time at such entertainment meccas as the newly created Atlantic City. The attraction of Florida as a vacation state was started when Henry Morrison Flagler built the first hotel of a future chain on Florida's east coast. Americans interested in preserving nature saw their dreams realized in the creation of new national parks like Yosemite and the Grand Canyon.

Physical fitness achieved a cult status by the late 19th century. The teachings of Friedrich Jahn led to the creation of gymnastic organizations called Turnvereins, which in turn stimulated the

I LOVE MY WIFE BUT OH YOU TYPEWRITER.

Around the turn of the century, it was the young female office worker, not the machine, who was known as the "typewriter." This photograph parodies the office romance.

concept of permanent daily exercise periods in the public school systems. Americans were encouraged to use such equipment as Indian clubs and beanbags to keep in shape. Health reformers such as

17

The sense of change in American life was made more real by the close connection to the past. As late as 1918, as Americans were fighting another war in Europe, New Yorkers were able to watch these Zouaves, aging veterans of the Civil War, march in remembrance of their sacrifice.

The vast wealth generated by the Industrial Revolution in the second half of the 19th century created a new class of American aristocrats, representatives of what Mark Twain called the "Gilded Age." Here a society woman poses for the photographer in her parlor.

John Harvey Kellogg, who would help to create the breakfast-food industry, influenced the way people ate. Whereas Americans in the 1860s ate heavy breakfasts, Kellogg advocated different types of cereals instead.

Hunting dogs on an estate at Newport, Rhode Island. Newport became a center for the summer mansions of many wealthy families at the turn of the century.

The desire for physical fitness stimulated athletic competitiveness, which promoted the rise of intercollegiate and professional sports. American pastimes like football and baseball achieved national commercial status. By the 1890s, baseball had evolved from a children's game to its professional form, quickly becoming the leading spectator sport in the country. The appearance of sports pages in the daily newspapers stirred the mania for sports records and statistics. Both the American and National Leagues were formed during this time. The sport of bare-knuckle prizefighting, epitomizing the ideal of male competitiveness, reached its pinnacle with such famed figures as John L. Sullivan and the black fighter Jack Johnson.

Fifth Avenue, New York, on Easter Sunday, 1900. All of the buildings along the Avenue in this picture, except for the church on the extreme right, were private residences owned by the Vanderbilt family.

21

Entertainment was not limited to the playing field. Roller-skating started in New York City in the 1860s and spread to the rest of the country within 10 years. Hardwood rinks were soon found in every town. The bicycle also made its appearance at this time—first as the "high-wheeler" (a vehicle with a large front wheel and a small back one) in the 1870s, and then as the modern bicycle with wheels of equal size in the mid-1880s. Hundreds of cycle clubs quickly followed.

Adult male workers had something else to occupy their time: the local saloon. Until Prohibition in 1920, the saloon was probably the most popular entertainment center for men in the late 19th century. The saloon had a dual purpose—it was a world away from the family and it was a hub for politics. The soda fountain was promoted as an alternative to the saloon. The ice-cream soda was created in 1874 by Robert M. Green. Soda waters and flavors were thought to have health benefits. Coca-Cola was concocted to cure headaches in 1886. Vaudeville theater houses, the predecessor to movies and television, brought live entertainment to less affluent neighborboods. Vaudeville became a stepping-stone to national fame for such stars as Will Rogers. As urban theater, vaudeville also became a mixing pot for ethnic communities. Municipal parks like New York's Central Park were built during this time as part of a movement to preserve nature in urban environments around the nation. Children's playgrounds came into being. The amusement park, a combination of industrial age gadgetry and the local fair, became a new form of weekend entertainment for the working-class communities of the cities.

Clothing and Fashion

REFLECTING THE INTERESTS AND INFLUENCES OF THE LATE 19th century, the world of clothes and fashion highlighted a varied spectrum of forms and functions. On one side, the affluence and progress of the age spurred the need for fashions that demonstrated people's social mobility—the costumes of the newly rich, the entrepreneur, and the advancing middle class. On the other side, the increase in the number of poorer immigrants made dress an ethnic melting pot of different designs and colors. People's interest in fashion was revolutionized by the appearance of the mail-order catalog and blue jeans.

One area in which fashion exhibited a rapid transformation was in the arena of work. As the workplace changed from the small craft shop to the big company, workers were expected to conform to a standard style of dress. From the 1870s to the turn of the century, business dress evolved from the Prince Albert long coat to the modern-day business suit, including the tie and the white collar shirt.

The business suit became the corporate ideal, a symbol of the modern male. For the laborer and factory worker, the ideal became the work uniform and union identification. The rise in labor consciousness gave special importance to denim overalls and the leather apron. Regulation wear became standard fare for government employees like postal workers and policemen. Women, too, did not escape the change in the work environment. Dressing for success in the new business office meant an organized and discreet look—a white shirtwaist and black skirt. Called "the Gibson Girl" style after artist Charles Gibson's well-known rendition of women in this era, it became popular primarily for its trendiness and practicality.

The growth of leisure time meant the need for comfortable dress. Clothes were designed around the requirement for lighter, more flexible wear in such activities as roller-skating, biking, and tennis. Riding togs, boating flannels, frocks, and gymnastic costumes were specially created. The turtleneck sweater was an offshoot of the biking craze. The promotion of vigorous exercise meant that Americans had become aware of their bodies. Swimming attire that covered most of the body was acceptable at the seashore. Although sports fashions of this age were prudish by modern standards, they still signified a greater freedom. Nowhere was this more apparent than in the changes in leisure wear for women. Women and girls were being liberated by recreational activities and sports. Bicycling made pants, divider skirts, and bloomer trousers on women respectable. By the 1890s, women were wearing biking outfits with knickers and caps that were criticized as improper, but the wheels of progress were already changing.

Before the 1880s, America was still a country of relatively regional interests. Small-town America was isolated from the trends of the big

A group of people on a summer excursion in the 1890s. The bowler and the straw hat had replaced the black stovepipe, at least for the middle class, but women's fashions were still very formal.

Searching for Easter eggs around 1900. The children of the wealthy were expected to present themselves as well dressed and carefully groomed and as models of propriety.

cities. The mail-order catalog, an innovation born in the 1890s, democratized American fashion. Symbolized by the best known of its breed—the Sears and Roebuck catalog—the mail-order book brought the latest in designs and fabrics to farm country and the small town. People everywhere, no matter how remote from urban centers, could now order the latest fashions. The early mail-order catalogs were still devoting more pages to home sewing needs than to ready-made wear. Yet the advent of mail order was significant: women could have manufactured, fashionable clothing delivered to their doors; men could buy hard-to-find tools; and children could discover the world of toys. Like the telegraph and the telephone, mail order brought Americans closer together.

Overalls, or denim trousers, were another by-product of this time. Originally designed with a high waist and straps to be used as protective work clothing, denim trousers would evolve by the 1890s into modern-day blue jeans. They were sold through mail-order catalogs and the general store and were merchandized in various colors and styles—some of which came to be identified with certain activities or with blue-collar work.

The decades of the 1870s to 1890s were ones of progress and opportunity. Men and women were influenced by the age of prosperity, anxious to show off their success or just frolic in the exciting new sports and games. The 19th-century male—symbolized by the self-made tycoon—was extremely conservative in his dress, reflecting a discreet promotion of wealth. At his side, dominating life at home and in society, was the American woman, pursuing life's finer things. Free from the troubles of adulthood were the children, dressed to fulfill the expectations of their parents.

Men's clothing was generally influenced by what was popular in England. In the early 1900s, the trend was toward tailed coats. Sloping down from the waist or square cut, jackets covered a high-collar shirt that was rolled over into lapels or straight cut. By the 1890s, the tailed coat had evolved into the morning coat with three buttons. The knickerbocker suit, also known as the Norfolk, was identified by its box pleats and large pockets. The most popular type of collar during this time, used with evening dress, was the wing collar. Trousers, which in the 1800s had an outward flare just above the foot, lost the flare and became somewhat loose fitting. Sporting clothes also imitated British designs. White was worn for cricket, boating, and tennis. By the 1880s, men wore white knickerbockers that stretched down to the calf, flat shoes, heavy stockings, and long-sleeved white jerseys as they swatted the ball over the net. The styles for formal wear varied from solid gray or black for the jacket to checks and stripes for the pants. Toward the 1890s, the patterns became more subdued, and the cut grew more sophisticated.

The most desirable hat fashion was the top hat. It dominated the entire 19th century for formal wear. The bowler hat made its appearance in the middle of the 19th century. It had a crown that was raised or lowered, according to fashion, by designers over the rest of the century. Another favorite in headgear was the Hamburg, or fedora. A felt hat noted for its dented crown and rolled brim, it reached its popularity in the last two decades of the 19th century when it was fashionable to wear it with another design statement of the time: tweed. For leisure wear, the modern American male wore the famed straw hat, used either as a sailor hat for the seaside or with a rigid brim and ribbon band for the famous barbershop quartets.

Proper attire for the beach in 1913 meant pantaloon-style bathing suits for women.

Through the 1860s and 1870s, large, thick sideburns—often leading down to the sides of the chin—were a common sight. Their popularity waned in the final decades, but they were replaced by enormous moustaches. Men were distinctively unflamboyant in their jewelry. Apart from gold or silver buttons, the most they might wear would be a gold watch chain.

29

In 1922, the city of Chicago had a law against women wearing abbreviated bathing suits at the beach. This photograph shows the new law being enforced.

For children, fashion trends were dictated by their parents and other adults, who were influenced by the increased interest in sports and a romanticized picture of how children should look. The type and length of a boy's trousers, for instance, would depend on his age—the older he was, the more likely he would be to wear adult clothes. A girl's age influenced the length of her skirt. The mail-order business, started in the early 1870s, gave boys everywhere the chance to wear cheap, factory-made clothes. The reintroduction of starch made even the most common girls' clothing crisp and clean.

A boy on display from the 1870s to the 1890s might wear exotic velvet or double-breasted wool dress suits. Instead of a shirt, he might wear blouse waists, which had long, full sleeves and a waistband fitted to be worn on the outside of the trousers. Collars were sometimes detachable. The zippered fly front was a new innovation for pants, although many trousers still had button fronts. Pleated at the waist, boys' trousers were somewhat baggy at the hips and gradually narrowed toward the feet. By the last decade of the century, two fashion innovations became important in boys' pants. First, suits had knee-length trousers, held up by buttons on the shirtwaist. Second, the custom of the crease began initially on fashionable men's clothes and then filtered down to boys' clothing.

At ease, boys anywhere could be found in plain shirts, with no detachable collar, a variety of vests, and homemade or hand-me-down pants. On their feet, they might wear anything from cowboy boots to high-top lace-up shoes or oxfords. If they were immigrant children, they might adorn themselves with a cap of some kind. Stocking caps, cowboy hats, and straw hats were popular. For fashionable leisure clothes, after the 1870s, the American boy chose items that resembled the new professional baseball uniform. Pants with knee britches were important for another reason. They were the first pants in the history of American fashion to have loops for the belt. The British sports suit made its debut in the 1870s for both men and boys. The jackets had four buttons; the trousers were trim. The lower legs were protected by canvas gaiters held on by metal clips, worn especially when biking or hiking. Boys of every age loved to wear leather-billed caps. Knickers became the newest fad. The jodhpur, a combination of knickers and leggings worn first by British troops in India, found its way into young male fashion in the 1890s. When the United States government started building new steamships in the 1880s, interest in sailor suits became the rage all over the country. Regulation naval wear was emulated by fashion designers.

A garden party at the New York Zoological Society in 1900. Informality of dress among these wealthy supporters of the zoo was not in evidence.

Pea coats and double-breasted sack coats or "reefers" became quite popular for boys.

The American woman, on the other hand, was still limited in her choice of fashions because of the need to demonstrate respectability and good breeding in polite society. Although she would start to emancipate herself by the beginning of the next century, she was still playing a second-class role to the assertive American male during the years 1870 to 1900. The expectations of the time were different for each gender: the man had to strive without question up the ladder to success while the woman had to pursue excellence in gentility. And while the man ruffled his feathers conservatively, the woman bared her plumage with conspicuous affluence.

It was important for a woman's dress to reflect the opulence of the age. She was expected to stand for proper behavior, social mobility, and cultural excellence. If the male image was associated with being rough and aggressive, the woman represented the finer things in life. The ideal of womanhood was sometimes a difficult one to follow, but at least the American female had fashion options from which to choose. The industrial age had created, if nothing else, the instruments of female fashion: the sewing machine, the corset, and the mail-order catalog.

Nothing distinguished the early dress of this period more than the appearance of the bustle. By the 1880s, it had become the fashion symbol of the era. Distinguished ladies everywhere climbed into this elaborate construction of wire and steel forms, stiffened gauze, horsehair, whalebone, and canvas. Protecting herself underneath with supports, covers, and petticoats, the genteel lady—bust pushed forward, hips thrown back—was ready to put on the crowning touch to this display, the dress.

A family group photographed on their back porch in 1910. This intriguing picture sets the severity of the period's dress against the warmth, closeness, and quiet dignity of the individuals in the group.

Designers had created different dress styles throughout the course of the century. Some of the variations included long, full skirts that trailed on the ground, high-waisted dresses, and overdresses

35

Celebrating the Fourth of July in 1906.

and overskirts that could be draped over the body and the bustle. One index of how the bustle affected a woman's body was that its suit-of-armor-like form practically dislocated the spine. By the end of the century, the bustle fell out of fashion.

The shoulders of women's clothing were puffed, waists were trimmed, and dress trains were allowed to extend from the rear. High necklines remained popular for day wear. Frills appeared like wings and were stiffened. Bold colors and reams of rich fabric were used. Hairstyles evolved from ringlets and coils in the 1870s to a conical coiffure in the 1890s. In the area of head wear, a lady might wear a straw hat, a small bowler, or a peaked cap. Topping this glamorous attire might be any assortment of beads, ruffles, bows, or laces. The whole ensemble—whether worn during the daytime or the evening—was designed to create the image of a stately, proper gentlewoman.

After the demise of the bustle, more attention was paid to the bodice and the area above the waist. Although dress skirts were styled simply, the sleeves became bigger and bigger until they appeared balloonlike in shape, finally puffing out in the last years of the 19th century. Women's outfits became more conservative to match the more businesslike demeanor of women as they entered the office world. Flowing lines and lighter fabrics became popular. The American woman discovered the advantages of the tailored suit, with its attractive but subdued design. As her role in American society changed, her fashion reflected that change.

The sewing machine made it easier to create dresses at home. Personal seamstresses were often employed, but the sewing machine was much faster. The appearance of mail-order catalogs brought the fineries of fashion and fabrics—in addition to a variety of other products—to rural America, helping to fulfill the fashion dreams of the country housewife.

Dress designs were varied for this period. When the fad was to explore how full skirts could become, they were pulled up into graduated folds. Sleeves were allowed to flare out at the lower arm. Lace-up boots became popular. High fashion brought out full-bodied dresses and tight upper-body attire. Aprons were created for the front of the clothes for practical protection. In the early 1880s, the princess dress became appealing because its lines fit the human form and flared out at the skirt. Even the influence of immigrant clothing styles and military uniforms affected some clothing designs. Nautical-style dresses with curved brimmed sailors' hats became a fashion item.

As physical education programs became more prevalent in schools, unique and functional clothes that allowed for more movement in gym classes were designed. Knickers, trousers, and culottes were popular for biking. Wool flannel bathing suits were introduced for the cold waters of lakes and springs as outdoor swimming for females became more acceptable. Ribbon hats, straw hats, and sunbonnets were seen on many girls for playtime. Long before it was seen on boys' clothes, the belt loop made its appearance on the fashions of young girls. By the late 1880s and early 1890s, divided skirts and bloomer trousers, because of their comfort, became popular for exercise, even though some adults felt they were unladylike.

As the century was coming to a close, clothing design and fashion styles were being influenced by the growth of big business and acceptable business attire, the increase in leisure time and sports activities, and the emancipation of the American woman from the restraints of a traditional society. Some of the styles—like the bustle—have lost favor and have never returned into popular taste. Others—like blue jeans, the turtleneck sweater, and the belt loop—have survived to this day and have become part of American culture.

Courtship and Marriage

THE IDEAL OF THE AMERICAN FAMILY IN THE YEARS AFTER the Civil War was highly traditional. The father was at the head of the family, ruling over his domain like some grand and mighty monarch. He was expected to slave away at his job so that his wife and children could live the life of affluence anticipated by the average middle-class family. The wife waited upon him dutifully when he came home, attending to his every need. His children called him "Sir" and were expected to obey the lord and master of the home. The father was the breadwinner for the family, working more than sixty hours a week, just so his doting brood could live the opulent new American lifestyle. The mother stayed at home, in charge of both the household and family finances. She oversaw the servants and controlled the family's cultural interests.

After the Civil War, the economy began to transform from one sustained by self-sufficient family farms to one based more on industry and trade. With the exception of the plantation economy in the South, society was becoming more urbanized. The Industrial

Revolution meant that individual fortunes could be made or lost at the drop of a hat. Panics and depressions could throw people out of work. It was not that the lives of the early farmers had not been precarious or full of hardship, but that the new urban lifestyle was full of new uncertainties and frustrations.

In response, Americans turned to the family. The family was the only place that the average Victorian American could find social order in the face of change—a set of rules and roles that could be relied on to provide stability. The family was tradition, the rock of Gibraltar, the anchor in a sea of flux. While the country was growing and changing at a tumultuous pace, the family gave both comfort and security. There was one big difference, however. This was not the family of the past. The growth of industry had created a new class of small business owners and professionals. Called the middle class, this class became dominant over the growing groups of immigrants and laborers, and they set the standards for the ideal family.

The middle-class family was governed by a strict set of rules and roles. Social rank was set by tradition. The man was superior to the woman and was given more opportunities. He could vote, enter politics, and go out into the world to work—if he was of the right social class. The male lived under a masculine code of behavior that expected him to conquer the world and acquire wealth. The woman, however, was obligated by tradition to raise a family and maintain a household. Not only was she not required to earn a living, but such an act would have actually interfered with her primary duties as a wife and mother. Women could neither vote nor have the same privileges of ownership. They could not move about as freely as men. Moreover, where men could be indiscreet, women were required to live within a complex ideal of feminine purity. By the end of the 19th

Courtship in the 1890s. Though the young couple was permitted to be alone, the parents or a chaperone were never far away in a proper household, and the ritual of getting to know each other was quite formal.

A formal 19th-century wedding portrait. The bride is wearing an elaborate gown with a floor-length veil.

century, however, these traditional roles and rules began to break down as women were given more opportunities in the workplace.

Before he could have a respectable Victorian family, an ambitious man had to court a virtuous woman. Late–19th-century standards for

The automobile opened up an entire new range of amusements. In particular, it allowed young couples to get away from their homes and spend more time together.

family life had created unique—if not amusing—rituals for wooing and winning over the opposite sex. Many of these rituals were the product of different religious backgrounds, nationalities, and social classes. Others were part of the teachings of influential marriage

This engraving shows a fashionable wedding in New York in the 1880s. Such events held great importance—they could indicate changes in ownership of the great fortunes of the wealthy or mark the promotion of new families into high society.

manuals that sprang up in this era. Authors passing themselves off as sage advisers recommended methods of courtship that might seem ludicrous today. For instance, young American men were cautioned not to marry before the age of 25 or they would weaken their bodies

45

A $10.00 BRIDAL SUIT FOR $4.75

Modeled from the French. It includes Gown, Skirt, Chemise, Drawers and Corset Cover. It is exquis-ite in pattern, perfect in detail, and withal a price wonder. If it only serves to introduce you to the liveliest store for Dry Goods in Chicago and the best Underwear Department west of New York, it will have answered a good purpose. We have a unique Catalogue for Spring—yours for the asking. Address

 **SCHLESINGER & MAYER, Chicago**

An advertisement from an early Chicago mail-order house featuring a complete set of bridal undergarments for $4.75.

and age prematurely. Their brains might clog and their nervous systems might become diseased—all because they had found the woman of their dreams before the proper age.

Young girls were no better off. Having to deal with a double standard, they fought hard to achieve the ideal of purity lest they be considered "impure" and "fallen." Depending on their social class, "lewd and lascivious behavior" might even be grounds for arrest. Young girls were advised not to read romantic novels, dance, write love letters to young schoolboys, stay up late, or drink hot drinks. Doctors said such behavior might lead to poor health, hysteria, and unreasonable excitement. Everything from personal hygiene to relationships with other girls was governed by this restrictive social code. Even schoolbooks that included racy material were banned.

Moral crusaders throughout the country urged parents to prepare their sons for manhood and protect their daughters' chastity. Young men were told to avoid hysterical females or those with small waists, as both indicated "premature decay." Small waists in women, said one author, often produced deranged children. Women were expected to seriously honor the request of any young man who wanted to check the bumps on her head for character defects. The practice was called phrenology and involved interpreting the shape of the head as a guide to personality traits and desires. Throughout the 1870s and 1880s, many marriage manuals promoted this unusual means of predicting compatibility. The sharp bachelor was one who had his head chart ready to match up to any prospective mate.

The era certainly had some remarkable suggestions for proper dating behavior. But in one way, the Victorian age was an improvement over the mid-18th century because romantic love was now acceptable as a reason for marriage. Affection between a man and a woman—at least among the middle class—was becoming just as important as social status or financial considerations. Undeniably, courtship was still under the authority of the male. A woman had to play a passive role, repressing any kind of emotion until she knew her suitor's marriage intentions. Strict modesty was advised, and a young woman was never to put herself in a compromising situation where she might be inappropriately kissed or have her hand held. Home and maternal thoughts came first. Only when the courting woman had found the right man could she return his love.

Even though the marriage manuals all advised against early marriage, the average Victorian woman actually got married about five years earlier than her counterpart in the late 1700s, at an average age of twenty-two as opposed to twenty-seven. Most marriage counselors taught that courtship should not begin before the early teens. A commitment to marriage, it was warned, should happen somewhere in the twenties but not later than thirty. These years in a young person's life fascinated the Victorians because it was at this time in history that adolescence was discovered as an important period in life. The stage between childhood and adulthood became the object of much research. One of the leading authorities in this area was G. Stanley Hall, who in 1904 published a thousand-page treatise that concluded that the teenage years were ones of romantic and idealistic uncertainty.

When girls were ready for courtship, there was a definite change in their appearance. Their mothers might note their eligibility by changing their hairstyle and dress style. No longer would they be costumed like children. Young eligible girls had to don the rigid corset that would mold the shape of their dress from adolescence to old age. Completing the transformation, young courting girls had

Men's and boys' fashions in the 1870s. While men's clothing grew more versatile during the last decades of the 19th century, female fashion was still restricted by society's demands of propriety, morality, and social mobility.

A picture postcard showing a courting couple during the early 1900s. Though courtship proceeded under strict rules of behavior, the 19th century marked the first time that romantic love was viewed as an acceptable reason for marriage.

A theatrical poster from the 1890s reflecting America's fondness for melodrama.

Courtship rituals of the Victorian era included the exchange of elaborate and sentimental greeting cards. The first commercial valentine cards appeared in the United States in the 1840s.

their hair pinned up and were clothed in a new conservative dress that conveyed the image of a proper young lady.

Many courting Americans were not quite sure how to behave with each other. So they obeyed the many books of social rules that were published at this time. Couples called each other "Miss" and

A wedding in Oregon in the early 1900s. Paper canopies of the type shown here were popular for weddings at this time.

"Mister" unless they had known each other for years. Eligible men and women communicated or made announcements through a complicated system of calling cards, left in the front halls of homes. Rules of etiquette strictly governed relationships.

But the Victorian era was not without its charm. A sentimental time, its courtships were full of lace-paper valentines, ruffles, and ribbons. Many activities were chaperoned, but couples could get away for some limited privacy, depending on where they lived. Country courters might arrange for a hayride or a sleigh ride or a boating trip on a lake. Their city cousins could break away for the adventure of a bicycle trip or a trolley excursion. A night on the town

A stereopticon slide for Valentine's Day, produced around 1910. Courtships of the period were full of flowers and sentimentality.

A family outing at the beach some time in the late 1890s. The strict morals of this era are reflected in the formality of the family's attire.

in the big city might mean a trip to the theater or the opera, topped off by a champagne dinner. Indoor games were popular, as were dances—much to the chagrin of some doctors—like the waltz and polka. Even though parents were warned about the dangers of high-spirited dancing, their sons and daughters could still be found kicking up their heels at country shindigs.

By the 1920s, the age of the "flapper," morals had loosened somewhat and public displays of affection were no longer unusual. Here a sailor and a marine kiss their sweethearts good-bye before shipping out.

A young man engaged in brisk wooing might whisper a few lines of poetry in the ear of his sweetheart in the moonlight. An interested woman might win her way to his heart—and his stomach—through her expertise in making sweets. Blushing at the right time and knowing when to act cavalier were all part of the art of Victorian courtship. The end result—marriage—also followed form and custom. The bride usually wore a colored dress rather than white. The groom dressed in a dark suit at the ceremony. They celebrated the event with a honeymoon at a resort like Niagara Falls. The honeymoon, primarily an institution of the middle class, became popular during this time and continues to this day. Another innovation that still survives was the bride's registry at the newly founded department stores. A custom that fit the needs of both young couples and customer-hungry retailers, the registry let friends of the bride know what gifts she wanted.

At the turn of the century, courting couples began to change their dating habits. Amusement parks, movies, and vaudeville shows replaced church socials and croquet matches as the places to go by 1910. The divorce rate also began to increase, with five times as many divorces in 1900 as there were in 1870. Traditional marriage and the ideal of the Victorian family were being challenged as not the only way of life for men and women.

In response, laws were passed in states to block this alarming trend. Many state legislatures raised the age of consent and narrowed the grounds on which divorce could be granted. Marital problems had become a concern of the state. The Victorian household was no longer the sacred domain of the male; women and children also had rights. Unique family courts were established to handle such matters as delinquency, desertion, separation, and child abuse. Even though the payment of alimony was practically unknown, some states were allowing breakups on the grounds of incompatibility.

The rise in divorce was a symptom of a much deeper ailment. Some tried to point the finger at the decline of family values or the stresses of everyday life. Far more important were the roles played by Victorian men and women. The dominating attitude of men in marriages became increasingly intolerant. Women were expected to live up to unrealistic standards. The restrictions placed on domestic and maternal roles limited freedom of expression. Women were beginning to sense that they were being denied basic civil rights and could not enjoy the same economic privileges as men. Being a housewife and mother was just fine, but there was more to life. The subservient role traditionally played by women became too much for many to bear.

The truth is that while many women were trying to maintain the image of the Victorian family, others were attracted to the growing women's rights movement and the increasing career opportunities in the workplace. The right to vote and the right to own property became important issues. The growth of the working class and the flood of new immigrants challenged the middle-class ideals of family. Employment in the world of business freed women from dependence on overbearing husbands. No longer fitted into the stereotype of helpless maidens who fainted at adversity, a "new woman" was emerging. Some were electing to go to college, some chose to remain single, and others pursued more nontraditional lifestyles. Although most women still wanted to be married, the very nature of family, courtship, and marriage—once sentimental and conservative— was being challenged.

Learning and Education

INSATIABLE CURIOSITY AND THE NEED TO ADAPT: THOSE
are two qualities that best characterize the culture of America
between the Civil War and World War I. The nation was expanding at
a tumultuous pace and Americans were hungry to learn about the
lives of those around them. The rate of progress had propelled them
from their familiar homes into uncertain destinies, from a state of
innocence into the rush of the future. Technological revolutions in
transportation, communications, and the economy fed the nation's
restless ego and made it hold a mirror up to itself to see what was
really happening.

　　People were worried that they would not be able to keep pace with
all this vast change. The revolutionary developments that were
happening in many sectors of society signaled a need for
self-awareness, new skills, and a better ability to stay afloat and keep
up. If citizens of the Victorian era were to succeed, they had to keep
current—if not one step ahead—of these incredible developments.
Those who were not open and aware were doomed to live in the past.

59

An 1881 woodcut satirizes schoolteachers who tried to cram their students' heads full of knowledge by rote memorization, as prescribed by local boards of education. That such a cartoon could appear indicates that people were rethinking the goals of education in order to produce more well rounded students.

The ones who were most vulnerable were those who had just arrived or those who were at the bottom of the ladder. Millions of new immigrants needed to adapt to American culture. The growing working class required training to advance beyond the barriers of poverty. Learning was more than simply curiosity—it was an absolute necessity in an age in which ignorance meant failure.

Learning came in many forms. In the formal sense, it flowered in the growth of the nation's public educational system. Revolutions in teaching expanded the ways in which American students were taught. Formal learning exploded in substance and scope. Curricula were reevaluated and redefined. More students went to school for a longer period of time than ever before. Kindergarten and high school programs were developed. New colleges and universities were established for a variety of needs. Correspondence schools emerged to make education available for the working class. Informally, America expressed and taught itself by first inventing and then making the best use of advances in technology and communications. The telephone and typewriter, once novelties, revolutionized the gathering of information. New printing presses bred mass newspapers and popular magazines. The camera fed the need for visual communication, eventually leading to the creation of the motion picture. Colorful novelists used the power of the word to define the American experience. Large expositions celebrated scientific and industrial progress and became a mecca for Americans to gather and marvel at their own greatness.

A challenging educational system was especially critical during an age in which change was so rampant. Educational leaders were fearful that antiquated programs could not keep up with the wheels of progress. How could schools best meet the requirements of a rapidly developing nation? How could education improve the lives of the millions of immigrants who were flowing into the country, anxious to find a common experience?

The number of people who were entering the schools had increased rapidly. The respect for learning, coupled with a growing

Between 1850 and 1880, it was common for teachers to issue Reward of Merit cards to outstanding students.

This cartoon from an 1878 New York newspaper makes the point that, in terms of salaries, teachers were worse off than school janitors. The janitors were well-paid political appointees.

This newspaper report from the late 19th century attempts to expose crowded, unsanitary conditions in New York City public schools. The public schools served the growing immigrant communities and were no better than the tenement housing the students commuted from every day.

DISEASE AND DEATH

The Public Schools Breed Cripples and Deformities.

SQUALOR AND FILTH THE RULE

The Children Losing Their Eyesight and Becoming Humpbacked---Curvature of the Spine the Prevalent Disease---That Beneficent Board of Education and its Splendid Work.

population, resulted in an increase in student enrollment in elementary schools from 7 million in 1870 to 16 million by 1900. High school enrollment almost quadrupled, and the number of students in colleges grew five times. Almost three-quarters of the nation's children were enrolled in elementary schools by the end of the century, and students were spending more time in the classroom. Primary education was still characterized by "reading, writing, and arithmetic," as taught by the perenially best-selling McGuffey's Eclectic Reader (more than 122 million copies of this book were sold between the 1830s and 1920s). But important changes were being made.

For one thing, city-school systems became better organized and developed eight-year programs. Although simple one-room schoolhouses still existed in the rural Midwest and Far West, urban educational systems revolutionized the very nature of schooling. Before the 1870s, primary education was haphazard and inefficient. Children stayed in school only until their families needed them to work. Teachers were poorly paid. Daily classes consisted of the basic fundamentals. There was a lot of memorization and recitation. The textbooks that were used were limited in scope and treated boys and girls unequally.

Once educational leaders recognized what had to be done, several important steps were made. Instruction was put on a graded level, so students could advance from one grade to another—replacing the old beginning, intermediate, and advanced grading system. Courses of study were standardized for all schools and all grades. Regular and orderly school attendance was required, eventually raising the age of compulsory education to the high school level. And school systems became bureaucratized, managed by superintendents and

The poet Walt Whitman fiercely defended Thomas Eakins and his efforts to promote realism in art, and he extolled the human form in his poetry.

principals and having precise roles for teachers. Topping it all off was the introduction of a new stage of childhood education, the kindergarten. First used in St. Louis in 1876, kindergarten was molded by the philosophy that very young children should have a class for themselves where play was encouraged more than interfering discipline. It became immensely popular.

An art education class in the late 19th century. Using live nude models was quite revolutionary in Victorian America. The renowned painter Thomas Eakins was dismissed from the Pennsylvania Academy of the Fine Arts in 1886 for insisting that his students paint from live nudes.

Because 19th-century parents were becoming increasingly interested in the "youth problem" posed by teenagers, if not the mystery of adolescence itself, secondary education took on a heightened importance during this period. Not wanting to see secondary education become the private preserve of elitist prep schools, leaders pushed for free high school education. Public funds were raised to build new high schools and to hire teachers

In the forefront of social criticism, as always, was the cartoonist Thomas Nast, who here satirizes sectarianism in the late–19th-century school system.

SECTARIAN BITTERNESS.

OUR COMMON SCHOOLS AS THEY ARE AND AS THEY MAY BE.—[See Page 141.]

Vaudeville theater—consisting of unrelated songs, dances, acrobatic and magic acts, and humorous skits—developed from the popular musical diversions of saloons. The rise of vaudeville houses across America during the 1880s brought affordable live entertainment to less affluent neighborhoods.

By the early 20th century, the American public school system had all but replaced one-room schoolhouses like the one depicted in this 1875 lithograph. Beginning in industrialized urban areas, American education became organized, graded, and standardized, and attendance through high school was compulsory.

An 1864 election poster. Overwhelming social and economic forces during the 19th century caused upheaval and corruption in the American political system. Although citizens decried the lack of principled leadership, more people than in any previous period of the country's history voted in presidential elections.

Extravagant political demonstrations such as this New York state election parade became common-place during the mid-19th century.

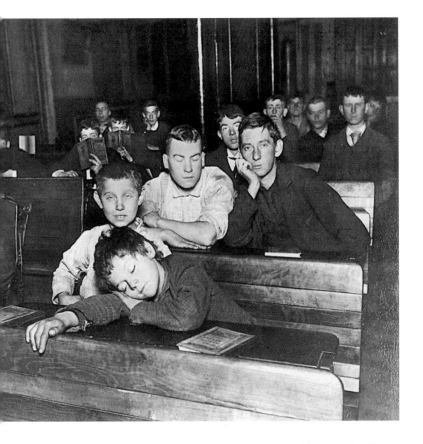

A schoolroom on the Lower East Side of New York City in 1886, photographed by the social reformer Jacob Riis.

trained through the state universities. Where before any education beyond the primary level was for the privileged male, schooling in the late 1800s was coeducational and more democratic. High schools had traditionally been thought of as preparation for college. Now they became places of vocational training leading to white-collar employment. Curricula became diversified and comprehensive. Above all, the high school was seen as a forum in which usefulness, moral values, and cooperation could be taught.

A teacher with her class in front of their sod schoolhouse in the Oklahoma Territory in 1895.

The typical teenager of 1900, ready for school.

Left to decline before the Civil War, higher education began to grow when Congress passed the Morrill Act in 1862. This law gave each state large tracts of federal land if, from the proceeds of the sale of that land, the states would establish vocational colleges in agriculture and the mechanical arts. Colleges for blacks and women began to appear. Imaginative college presidents like Andrew White of Cornell and Charles Eliot of Harvard transformed their campuses from schools dominated by the ancient classics to educational centers with flexible programs and new areas of study. Higher education became a requirement for those wishing to enter law, medicine, or teaching.

Throughout the country, the exchange of information was accelerated by important advances in technology. The telephone was first marketed to the public in 1878, and by 1900 more than 1.5 million phones were in operation. Unlike the telegraph, the telephone did not require the learning of a special code to communicate. Person-to-person communication was immediate and intimate.

The typewriter also revolutionized the working environment. First exhibited at the Philadelphia Exposition in 1876, the typewriter sped up the recording and printing of information. Through typing schools set up by typewriter companies, women broke into the white-collar work force.

High-speed printing presses, also developed during this period, fostered the growth of mass newspapers and popular magazines that would mold public opinion. Many small tabloids, lacking in color and excitement, became mass publications, printing as many as 10 editions a day. In addition to the news, special sections were devoted to coverage of sports, travel, and women's issues, and crossword puzzles and comics made their appearance. Competition for the best stories and the most readers became intense. Human-interest and advice columns became popular. Innovations in woodcut and steel-engraved illustrations promoted the use of colorful graphics. Magazines such as the *Ladies Home Journal* and the

Saturday Evening Post flourished at this time, helped by declining mail rates and lower costs in paper manufacturing. These magazines not only promoted consumerism through advertising but reinforced the tastes and values of the rising middle class.

By the 1890s, newspapers had reached their zenith. The fierce competition for news stories produced the phenomenon of "yellow journalism," where editors would approve the inclusion of fictionalized or sensationalized writing in news stories to keep the readers hanging on every word. Political cartoonists became

A typical early–20th-century classroom. The teacher is discussing Indian lore.

very popular, among them Thomas Nast, who also created the modern image of Santa Claus.

The culture of the late 19th century was altered by other inventions—the phonograph, the camera, and the motion picture. Now people could make a permanent and accurate record of their experiences. The phonograph, invented by Thomas Edison, made possible the growth of the recorded-music industry. With the development of roll film and dry-plate developing, amateur photography became a national hobby. Family photograph albums gave people a stronger sense of identity and continuity with past generations. Movies first appeared in the 1890s, beginning as primitive kinetoscopes. Silent films were shown with live piano accompaniment in neighborhood theaters.

Advances in electrical engineering had brought artificial light into households, expanding the types of activities people could engage in during the evening hours. People were conscious of the fact that they lived in a machine age and that such an age would be characterized by progress and rapid change.

Politics

WRACKED BY THE INCREDIBLE SPEED OF TECHNOLOGICAL change and the complexity of the issues and problems confronting it, the political system of the United States in the 19th century underwent a dramatic upheaval. The social and economic forces of the era turned a political system used to men of vision like Washington and Jefferson into a system that was satirized for its corruption, patronage, and inefficiency, and which was generally held in low regard by the public. The idealism of the past was gone.

From the very beginning of the Victorian age, politicians were little respected. In 1869, a Cabinet member was quoted as saying: "You can't use tact with a Congressman! A Congressman is a hog! You must take a stick and hit him on the snout!" To which someone else replied: "If a Congressman is a hog, what is a Senator?" This kind of talk signaled a theme that was echoed time and again from the Civil War to the 20th century: the lack of principled leadership. With issues such as war, union, and slavery no longer pressing, American politics began to put more emphasis on show than on substance, and on elections that were popularity contests rather than contests of principles. Political machines and party bosses appeared, and everyone was caught up in the fast money and the quick fortunes that could now be made.

Of course, there were some exceptions to the trend. In 1872, Victoria Woodhull became the first American woman to run for the presidency, and Susan B. Anthony cast the first vote by a woman in a

Bringing older voters to the polls, from an 1874 woodcut.

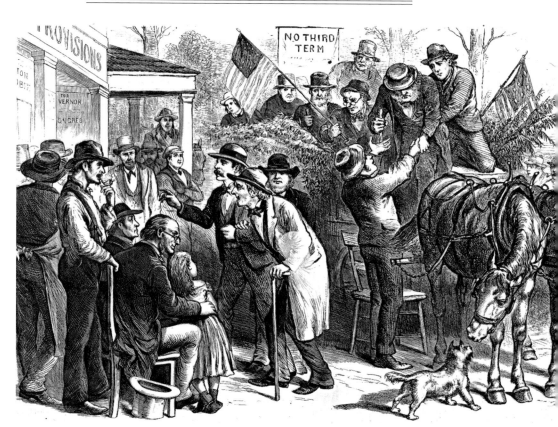

national election—for which she was arrested. Noted abolitionist Frederick Douglass became the first black to be nominated for president at the Republican National Convention of 1888.

In general, however, this was not the age of honest or idealistic politics. Because so many were finding fame and fortune in business, and because a well-placed public servant might personally profit from aiding or protecting the arrangements of businessmen, the public began to take a low view of politicians. No president between Grant and McKinley was ever reelected by the public after his first term in office. In the same time period, no presidential candidate ever received a majority of the popular vote. Control of both houses of Congress changed hands repeatedly, no president had a party majority in both houses for a complete term, and the party majorities that did exist were razor thin. The great thinkers and doers of the time were drawn into fields other than public office.

With few men of ideas and convictions to march behind, political parties became dependent on machine politics, fund-raising, campaign hoopla, and demagogic speech making to win the public's attention. Broadsides, symbols, songs, slogans, and other paraphernalia bombarded the citizenry. During campaigns, political parties held huge torchlight parades that lasted for hours. Candidates even let their likenesses be used on advertisements for household products. The Republican elephant and Democratic donkey were born during the campaign of 1876, and the Republicans started calling themselves the "Grand Old Party" in the election of 1880.

In the Victorian age, the biggest influence on public opinion was the spoken word. When all else failed, speech making and political rallies were used to whip up public support, and those who were

The interior of a polling booth, around 1860.

eloquent and spellbinding were most in demand. The most notable American example of the Victorian political speech maker was William Jennings Bryan. Bryan set the precedent for aggressive campaigning in 1896, traveling farther to see more people than any other presidential candidate before him. In one day alone, he gave 36 speeches. He was given to eating six times a day and chomping on buckets of radishes to keep up his energy.

Until the last decades of the 19th century, it was somewhat taboo for a candidate—especially someone already in office—to personally involve himself in campaigning. Going on the stump, as it were, was

A 1900 campaign poster for Republican candidate William McKinley.

There is perhaps no greater obscurity than the obscurity that overtakes failed presidential candidates. Here are two completely forgotten names from history, Alton B. Parker and Henry G. Davis, the Democratic presidential and vice presidential candidates for the 1904 election, which was won by Theodore Roosevelt running on the Republican ticket. The 1904 election also featured candidates for the Populist and Prohibition parties, as well as a socialist candidate, Eugene V. Debs.

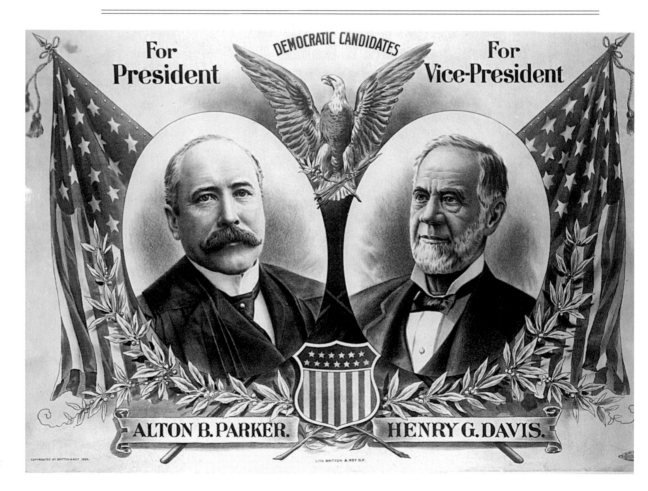

left to underlings. Grant did not campaign at all and still won the election. Garfield campaigned from his front porch in 1880. He and his wife greeted voters of all types from their home in Mentor, Ohio, and served them lemonade. Cleveland campaigned only twice in 1884 and won.

The politician's nemesis was the press, especially as exemplified in the political cartoon, used in both magazines and newspapers. America's best-known Victorian political cartoonist was Thomas Nast, who worked for *Harper's Weekly*. The same artist who was to create the first modern illustration of Santa Claus in 1881, Nast invented the animal symbols that became identified with the two major political parties. A brilliant artist who used his sharp pencil to satirize the corruption of his time, Nast became the role model for future editorial cartoonists.

One of the best-known examples of Nast's work appeared during the second administration of Ulysses S. Grant. The largest city in the country, New York, was embroiled in a major corruption scandal. William M. "Boss" Tweed of Tammany Hall had been stealing from the taxpayers through the use of fraud and kickbacks. Millions of dollars had gone through his hands. Nast helped expose Tweed to the public through severely critical cartoons and aided in bringing about Tweed's downfall. In the election of 1872, Nast took on Horace Greeley, the founder of the New York Tribune, who was running against Grant. He pictured him as wishy-washy and without principles; another New York newspaper characterized the whole campaign as a "shower of mud." Nast's rival, the political cartoonist Matt Morgan, made Grant out to be an incompetent drunk in his cartoons. By the last decade of the 19th century, political cartoons had become fixtures in journalism.

While Mark Twain named the late 19th century the "Gilded Age," the writers Henry James (left) and Edith Wharton (opposite page) explored the customs and manners of the rich in their novels.

Of course, the politicians were not without their weapons too. The end of the Victorian age signaled the beginning of the professionally run campaign. In 1896, the presidential campaign of William McKinley became the first instance of the mass marketing of a

Buying voters in Tennessee in 1895.

candidate. McKinley was guided by a powerful Cleveland businessman named Mark Hanna. Hanna used his business expertise to raise both money and support for his protégé. Over $7 million was raised by Hanna through financial connections and corporations. He quickly became McKinley's campaign manager and the "boss" of the party. Although they had a feisty opponent in William Jennings Bryan, Hanna and McKinley had a plan. McKinley did not want to travel, so Hanna had thousands of supporters trucked into Canton, Ohio, to pay respects to the man as he stood at his front porch. Next, Hanna assembled a small army of silver-tongued speakers to rally enthusiasm on McKinley's behalf. Campaign literature was mailed out by the millions and more people voted than ever before.

In McKinley's 1900 campaign, so much money was raised that the Standard Oil Company actually had a part of its contribution refunded. Vice presidential candidate Theodore Roosevelt covered 21,000 miles in eight weeks on McKinley's behalf. Fate was to play the final hand, however. McKinley was assassinated by an unemployed anarchist as he was shaking hands at the Pan-American Exposition just eight months after the election.

As running a presidential campaign became more complex, politics became more financially demanding. The Republicans spent $150,000 on Grant's first campaign. In the 1876 campaign, the Republicans were said to have spent $950,000 and the Democrats $900,000. In 1888, the Republicans raised almost twice as much as the Democrats ($1,350,000 versus $855,000). The Democrats reversed this in 1892 by spending $2,350,000 against the Republican's $1,700,000. In his last election in 1900, McKinley had over $3 million in his campaign chest. The raising of all this money required skillful financial dealing. It also opened the door to political corruption and the domination of the

Women voting in a municipal election in Boston in the late 19th century. Women in all states did not obtain the right to vote in national elections until after the First World War.

political process by special-interest groups. As the coffers bulged with funds, political ethics became more flexible.

The administration of Ulysses S. Grant, especially, was criticized for being more corrupt than any administration before or since—largely because of political incompetence and scandals. Mark Twain

The corrupt New York City commissioner William "Boss" Tweed is investigated by city aldermen in 1871.

called the post–Civil War period the "Gilded Age" because it was filled with con artists and robber barons, all anxious to take advantage of a healing nation. In 1872, two congressmen and Vice President Schuler Colfax were implicated in the Crédit Mobilier

After his indictment for forgery and bribery, Tweed escaped from jail in 1875 and fled to Cuba. But someone who had seen cartoonist Thomas Nast's caricatures of Tweed spotted him and pointed him out to authorities, and he was rearrested.

SHERIFF'S OFFICE

OF THE CITY AND COUNTY OF NEW YORK.

December 6th, 1875.

$10,000 Reward.

The above reward will be paid for the apprehension and delivery to the undersigned, or his proper agents, of

WM. M. TWEED,

Who escaped from the Jailor of the City and County of New York, on Saturday, December 4th, 1875. At the time of his escape he was under indictment for Forgery and other crimes, and was under arrest in civil actions in which bail had been fixed by the Court at the amount of Four Million Dollars.

The following is a Description of said WM. M. TWEED:

He is about fifty-five years of age, about five feet eleven inches high, will weigh about two hundred and eighty pounds, very portly, ruddy complexion, has rather large, coarse, prominent features and large prominent nose; rather small blue or grey eyes, grey hair, from originally auburn color; head nearly bald on top from forehead back to crown, and bare part of ruddy color; head projecting toward the crown. His beard may be removed or dyed, and he may wear a wig or be otherwise disguised. His photograph is attached.

WILLIAM C. CONNER,
Sheriff.

scandal when they were found with mysterious stock certificates. Illicit profits were obtained by officials in the government from the Whiskey Ring. And President Grant's brother-in-law was involved in a gold scam thought up by "Jubilee Jim" Fisk and Jay Gould, both millionaires. Some thought the democratic system had finally hit rock bottom and the machinery of government was falling apart.

Political campaigns themselves became mired in the worst kind of mudslinging and name-calling. Part of the decline in the status of politicians can be attributed to the demise of personal respect. Instead of concentrating on the issues, campaigns became a battle of personalities and investigations into the personal conduct of the candidates. Grant was called a drunk and a fool. Greeley, who helped start the Republican party in 1854, was ridiculed for his appearance—steel-rimmed spectacles, white coat, tall white parson's hat—and for his eccentric causes like free love and vegetarianism. Grover Cleveland was accused of having sired an illegitimate child—to which he admitted. Benjamin Harrison was the "human iceberg." William Jennings Bryan was an "anti-Christ" and a "madman."

What the American public saw as lacking in its politicians of the time was courage and character. The occupation seemed precarious and without prestige. Many representatives in Congress were first-termers, and they made far less money than their brethren in industry. Instead of debates over ideals, elections became fierce contests over personal character. Political parties hesitated to take firm positions on controversial questions. The president and Congress were seen as ineffective, which made it difficult for voters to identify with one party or the other. Congress was ridiculed in the late 1880s for its inability to handle itself, and editorials called it "Slowly Doing Nothing."

Yet in spite of all these problems, the American public was still interested in the political process. More people voted in presidential elections than in any previous period. Closely fought elections were watched down to the wire. The electorate quickly gobbled up the lastest in journalistic gossip. All the words and political hoopla found an eager audience around the country. Recognizing that the system, like the country, was undergoing tremendous change, it was almost as if the public had not quite given up hope. Or perhaps, as others have suggested, politics had become the latest national pastime, rivaling baseball or basketball for stimulation. What better way to get emotionally involved than through a close election. It was politics as theater. The fact that the public had not yet abandoned the political process was testament not only to the democratic system but also to the colorful nature of politics itself.

FURTHER READING

Clark, Judith Freeman. *America's Guilded Age*. New York: Facts on File, 1992.

Cremin, Lawrence. *American Education: The Metropolitan Experience, 1876–1980*. New York: Harper and Row, 1988.

Garraty, John. *The New Commonwealth*. New York: Harper and Row. 1978

Ginger, Ray. *An Age of Excess: The United States from 1877 to 1944*. New York: MacMillan, 1965.

Haller, John, and Robin Haller. *The Physician and Sexuality in Victorian America*. New York: W. W. Norton, 1974.

Jones, Howard. *Age of Energy: Varieties of the American Experience*. New York: Viking, 1970.

Kidwell, Claudia, and Margaret C. Christman. *Suiting Everyone: The Democratization of Clothing in America.* Washington, D.C.: Smithsonian Institution Press, 1975.

May, Elaine Tyler. *Marriage and Divorce in Post-Victorian America.* Chicago: University of Chicago Press, 1980.

Neil, Harris, ed. *The Land of Contrasts: 1880–1901.* New York: Doubleday, 1970.

Rothman, Ellen. *Hands and Hearts: A History of Courtship in America.* Cambridge, MA: Harvard Press, 1987.

Schlereth, Thomas J. *Victorian America: Transformations in Everyday Life, 1876–1915.* New York: HarperCollins, 1991.

Sullivan, Mark. *Our Times: The Turn of the Century.* Vol. 1. New York: Scribner's, 1971.

Worrell, Estelle. *Children's Costume in America. 1607–1910.* New York: Scribner's. 1980.

Yellowitz, Irwin. *The Position of the Worker in American Society.* Englewood Cliffs, NJ: Prentice Hall, 1969.

INDEX

PICTURE CREDITS

JIM BARMEIER, a native of Chicago, received a bachelor's degree from Denison University in Ohio and a master's degree from Stanford University in California. A member of the Writer's Guild of America, he has written several produced episodes of cartoon series including "Smurfs" and "Defenders of the Earth." He currently works as a creative consultant in the Los Angeles area.

...lars. Same
...y imported
...w and hand-
...ds; stripes,
...tal fancies
...of colorings.
...man will
.....**$1.30**

...and medi-
...mbinations.
..., Persians,
...figures and
...reds, wines,
...ng shades.
...ice. Don't
...t tie of the
.........**38c.**

...WS.
...r.
...e New Pull
...e of French
...viot, in **50**
...ns, checks,
...t and dark
...lastic band
...vable ends,
...gthened or
...esired. The
...ng, neatest
...er ⅓ dozen
Pointed or
a.........**75c.**

...VS.
...r.
...ows. Fine
...ely new and
...colors, **100**
...en.....**65c.**

Scarfs.

...2282.
...3. Pure
...Club House
...ntirely new
...ncluding
...vel and at-
...mbinations.
...Dresdens,
...ncy figures
...al designs,
...f charming
...ive styles.
...lacks or
...Remember
...are pure

No. 21575 Children's Fancy Parasols. Made in new and beautiful patterns; light colors, like pink, blue, etc. Size, 10 inch...**$0.17**

Size, 12 inch..............**.22**
Size, 14 inch.............**.33**
No. 21576 This is an exceptionally nice Misses' Sateen Parasol; 14 inch, plain solid colors, with ruffle, fancy stained and polished handles; colors, pink, cardinal, white, or blue.
We offer this at an exceptionally low price, and guarantee it to give perfect satisfaction.
Our special price.............**$0.48**

Misses' Fancy Foulard Pattern Paarasol.

No. 21577 Large choice assortment of handsome patterns; floral and dresden designs, etc., new and beautiful colorings. Nicely made and finely finished throughout; natural wood handles. Our special prices,
14 inch..............**$0.50**
16 inch.............**.76**

THIS IS A VERY HANDSOME
16 IN. MISSES'
FANCY FOULARD... PATTERN PARASOL.
No. 21578 with a beautiful star ruffle of satin, corresponding in color to that of the parasol. Handsome shades of light blue and pink. Newest fancy patterns; natural wood han-
dles; nicely made and finished.
Our special price.............**87c**

THIS IS AN
EXCEPTIONALLY FINE....
MISSES' PURE ...SILK...
PARASOL.
No. 21579 Has deep flounce and puff. Extra fine quality natural wood sticks. Size 14 inch. Made in plain colors only; pink, blue and cardinal. Extra made and nicely finished. Guaranteed to please the most sceptical.
Our Special Price.............**$1.10**

IF THE COST OF THE BOY'S CLOTHING

SCARFS.
See our special half-dozen offer. It will pay you to lay in a supply for yourself and friends.
No. 2224. Men's Fine Fancy Silk Teck Scarfs. The kind that you usually pay 35c, 45c, and 50c for. Our price is a revelation. We buy these goods direct, thousands of dozens at a time, and all the year around. These scarfs are made from fine quality imported fancy silks. We have them in checks, stripes, dots, neat figures, and imperial designs, medium and dark combination colors. No plain black or white. All nicely made and trimmed. Surprising values, every one of them. Our special price, each.........**19c**; Six for......**$1.00**

Silk Folding or String Ties.

Fancy Figured Silk String Ties.
No. 2225. Medium width, assorted, dark or medium colors, nicely made and finely finished folded string ties.
Per dozen.... 2.50 Price, each. ..**$0.23**

Black Silk Folded Ties.

Known as string ties, made of pure gros grain silks, extraordinary values in each number; this is a tie that can be worn on all occasions, and especially suitable for elderly gentlemen.
No. 2226. ⅝ inch wide....14c each...6 for **$0.80**
No. 2227. ¾ " " ...18c each..6 for **1.00**
No. 2228. ⅞ " " ...22c each..6 for **1.25**
No. 2229. 1 " " ...27c each..6 for **1.55**
No. 2230. 1¼ " " ...30c each..6 for **1.75**

Hot Weather Neckwear. An untied man is ever an untidy man. No chance for untidiness here. Ours is a tide of low prices and should be taken at the flood.

Gentlemen's Silk Bow Ties.

For turn-down Collar.
No. 2232. Fancy Silk Bow Ties for 6 cents, with shield for turn-down collar. Any of this lot of ties would cost you a quarter in any retail store. There is nothing old or off-color; everyone is as handsome as can be: all full size, pretty fancy colors; made of remnants of silks. We have contracted to take all the largest manufacturer of neck ties in New York will have for the entire season. They are made from remnants left from high grade ties, and are a bargain.
Each.....................**6c**
¼ doz., assorted.........**30c**
No. 2246. Black Silk Bows, with shield and elastic loop for turn-down collar.
Each......**10c**; ½ dozen, for.....**50c**
No. 2250. Men's Fine Black Satin Bows, with shield and elastic loop, for turn-down collars. Extrafine selected stock. Price, each........**10c**; 6 for..........**50c**

Black Band Bows.

For Standing Collar.
No. 2251. Black Bow. Popular wedding tie, fine grade satin and silk. Each.... ..**15c**
Half doz......................**80c**
No. 2252. Same as above, only pure white. Each. ..**15c**

No. 2251.

Half doz.........**80c**
No. 2254. Senator Band Bow. Extra quality silk or satin, latest shape, with patent band clasp at back so it can be worn with standing collar. Plain black only.
Each... ....**15c** Half dozen.........**80c**

White China Silk Band Bows.

No. 2255. Men's Extra Fine Pure White China Silk Band Bows for standing colars.— The daintiest

And...
No...
Bon...
Fau...
has a...
chif...
of...
folla...
and...
with...
satin...
satin...
Ea...

LADIES' MOURNING BONNET.

No. 23479 We show in this illustration a very handsome Bonnet and Mourning Veil. It is made exactly like the cut, of extra quality material. We offer it as an especial bargain and its actual value is at least 50 per cent. above our prices if bought in retail stores.
Our special price.......**$2.98**

NOTE.—When ordering trimmed [] tion color that is wanted.

Untrimmed Hat

Our Line of Untrimmed Hats []
complete at the beginning of a se[]
now. We have everything that is []
and the prices are lower than ever. []
member that many a dollar can be []
your hats of Sears, Roebuck & Co.

No. 23481 Children's Straw Sail[] around band and ribbon streame[] Colors, navy, brown, cardinal and [] is usually sold by retail merchants [] Our special price, each...........

No. 23483 Charlotte, a new stra[] but made of a rough straw; this hat [] lonable this spring. Colors, black, [] Each..................

No. 23484 Ladies' Black or W[]